ENGLISH HISTORY, 1815-1914

By R. K. WEBB

Columbia University

English History, 1815–1914

By R. K. WEBB

Although historical knowledge does not become obsolete as rapidly as knowledge in medicine and the sciences, it certainly does not stand still. In nearly any historical field, a teacher's working bibliography today will contain few books published longer than twenty years ago. Older studies that have kept their place—because they rank as classics or because they have been seminal for subsequent work—must often be subjected to considerable criticism and correction. Given this "permanent revolution," it is comforting to be able to begin this essay by referring to a classic and seminal work that remains authoritative and indispensable, even though some of it is now more than fifty years old.

Élie Halévy's *A History of the English People in the Nineteenth Century* (1913–1932, translated 1924–1934, with a posthumous volume, 1947) is incomplete: the first four volumes, the last only partly finished, cover the period from 1815 to 1852; the two-volume epilogue deals in somewhat more detail with the two decades from 1895 to 1915, a period in which Halévy knew England at first hand and about which his deep interest in the First World War compelled him to write out of sequence. But even in its truncated form, the work is one of the few undoubted masterpieces of historical scholarship, magnificent as narrative, brilliant as analysis.

It has often been remarked that Halévy's *History* displays a kind of objectivity and a clarity that seem peculiarly French; it has less often been recognized that its special virtues reveal a quality of mind that grew out of Halévy's training as a philosopher. This predisposition led Halévy to work out the firm structure of ideas that underlies the *History* and that helps to explain its permanence, whatever errors in fact may be found or whatever criti-

1

cisms of interpretation may be made. It also committed Halévy
to his characteristic emphasis on the history of ideas; indeed the
most striking contribution of the *History* is to draw attention to
the role of ideas, and of religion in particular, in determining the
course of English development. This emphasis is clearest and most
rewarding in the first volume, *England in 1815*. There, by way of
an analysis of English society at the end of the Napoleonic Wars,
Halévy seeks to answer the question why England did not un-
dergo a revolution of the kind that so sharply deflected the history
of his own country and that, on nearly any showing, should have
occurred in England as well. Halévy found the key to the puzzle
in the diversion of crucial and potentially revolutionary segments
of English society away from politics into evangelical religion,
particularly Methodism. This hypothesis has often been attacked,
and some valuable corrections have been made, but it remains a
challenging interpretation that can by no means be dismissed as
outdated or wrong.

Halévy's emphasis on religion merges, however, into a larger
concern with the liberal tradition of which England is the exem-
plar; indeed, the *History of the English People* forms one side of a
major dichotomy in Halévy's work, the other side being the history of socialism. Halévy's interpretation of English liberalism
drew on his vast and still authoritative analysis of the Benthamite
strain in English thought in his *The Growth of Philosophic Radicalism* (1901–1904, translated 1928). He saw Benthamism, with
its emphasis on state intervention, as interacting with the com-
plementary yet opposing laissez-faire tradition exemplified by the
classical economists descending from Adam Smith. By mid-century these two strains had fused, but not in equal proportion:
"Manchester" had triumphed over "Westminster," Smith over
Bentham, the natural over the artificial identification of interests,
freedom over coercion, the marketplace over bureaucracy. A reformed and newly efficient coercive state was being formed, and
in the late Victorian period was to become more and more the
principal engine for implementing changes in social policy. But
as men saw things in the 1850's, the state remained subordinate,
an administrative necessity in a society that was liberal and in-
dividualistic, not bureaucratic and collectivist. Sir Robert Peel,

prime minister in 1834-1835 and again during 1841-1846, best
exemplifies this amalgam of the liberal and the administrative
genius. Peel stands, quite properly, as Halévy's "hero," a place he
probably still holds for most historians of the Victorian Age.

In contrast to the pacific, liberal England of Peel and John Stu-
art Mill—Mill would, no doubt, have figured more fully in the volumes Halévy was unable to write—stood the rambunctious liberalism of the foreign policy of Canning and Palmerston, which
Halévy came more and more to distrust. He did not like to write
about foreign policy, he said, because ultimately foreign policy
meant war; and war in 1914-1918 made it clear how far the balance in England had been tipped away from liberalism toward
collectivism. In the postwar world, looking beyond England to
Europe, Halévy gloomily predicted the final submergence of
freedom in authority and the opening of a new "era of tyrannies."
The structural and interpretative relevance of this larger anti-
thesis between the liberal and the authoritarian has been less ap-
preciated than Halévy's contributory arguments about Methodism
and Benthamism; but it may offer one avenue for future reinterpretation of the history of nineteenth-century England.

Halévy's *History* is, then, a work with which teachers and stu-
dents must inevitably begin and to which they will repeatedly
return. Yet our knowledge of the nineteenth century has expanded
in many different directions, so much so as to make irrelevant most
general accounts written before the Second World War and to
falsify many old generalizations still found in textbooks and class-
rooms. It is impossible in a brief essay to deal even-handedly with
all aspects of a century that, in English history at any rate and possibly in all history, is unexampled in its richness of texture and its
complication of change and survival. Professor W. L. Burn has
recently drawn attention to a game all historians of nineteenth-
century England play, consciously or unconsciously; he calls it
"selective Victorianism"—making what one wants from the century's variety and resistance to comprehensive analysis. Our understanding of the century is dependent, willy-nilly, on what historians
have written about it, and recent historiography has developed
unevenly. One can speak with considerable confidence about certain aspects of the nineteenth century; about others one must re-

main nearly silent. This imbalance in our knowledge dictates that the bulk of this essay will deal with the structure and substance of politics, and the nature of the society reflected in politics. Those are the areas about which we know most and in which we can find more or less agreement. Following closely, and in some respects surpassing our political knowledge in its "hardness," is the field of economic history, which will receive somewhat less space here only because a more than summary treatment would require moving to a completely different level of analysis beyond the scope of this essay and possibly the competence of its author. At the end, very brief consideration will be given to intellectual history. The bonds that tie its practitioners to professional historians have grown steadily more tenuous, in England at any rate. Until a new integration is found between ideas, institutions, and social movements, intellectual history can command no more than marginal attention in a general survey.

The Structure of Politics

The constitutional and political history of nineteenth-century England will always be a commentary to some degree on the three installments of parliamentary reform in 1832, 1867, and 1884–1885. Each of these reforms expanded the electorate and recast the parliamentary map; each of them was in a way revolutionary. But the nature of these revolutions has been drastically reinterpreted, and the relationship of one reform act to another has been greatly complicated. To some extent the Reform Act of 1832— "The Great Reform Bill," as it used to be called—has been dethroned from its eminence. Its passage left no doubt that what the country wanted it would get or that the House of Commons, which represented the country, was supreme in the constitution. Thus the act symbolizes the destruction of the classical "balance of the constitution," achieved, as the eighteenth century understood it, by dividing power among king, lords, and commons. Opposition in the House of Lords to the Reform Bill had made the Lords the target of bitter attacks, and some enthusiastic radicals predicted its early extinction; but it was the independent executive power of the king that suffered most in the aftermath of 1832. The king's political power had been on the wane since the first premiership of the younger William Pitt (1783-1801) and George III's with-drawal from active participation into madness. But when William IV, exercising what had once been an undoubted prerogative, dis-missed his Whig ministers in 1834, Peel's Conservative govern-ment was defeated in the general election in 1835; the result showed that a government's "responsibility" ran to the House of Commons and ultimately to the electorate, not, as in the eight-eenth century, to the king.

For another generation, though, men continued to talk about the balanced constitution; only in 1867 did Walter Bagehot, in his brilliant essay *The English Constitution,* make the transformation plain by distinguishing between the monarchy and the House of Lords as the "dignified" elements of the constitution and the House of Commons and the government as its "efficient" elements. This is not to say that in 1834 or 1867 the monarchy or the House of Lords ceased to be important. The Lords caused trouble to the Commons throughout the century. By the early twentieth century the upper house was frankly obstructionist; hence the Parliament Act of 1911 converted its absolute into a suspensive veto. So too the monarchs—Victoria, Edward VII, and George V—retaining what Bagehot defined as "the right to be consulted, the right to encourage, the right to warn," remained a constant (sometimes more bothersome than helpful) factor in ministerial calculations. But interesting though kings and queens may be to general read-ers, they hold no central place in the thinking of historians. After 1837, only Prince Albert, the Prince Consort, retains real signifi-cance; able, dedicated, scientifically inclined, and essentially mod-ern, Albert presents the tantalizing question of what might have happened had he not died young in 1861. Symbolism and her name aside, it is impossible to ask such a question about Victoria's dying early; in the business of historians today, her son and grand-son count for even less.

No one would speak with any confidence today, as historians once did, of the Reform Act of 1832 as the statute that brought the middle classes into political power. The expansion of the elec-torate, to be sure, gave the vote to what Macaulay called the "vast masses of property and intelligence"; but historians are now im-pressed by the high degree of continuity that characterized poli-

tics, both at the center and in the localities, before and after the
Reform Act. This continuity survived even the dose of real democracy injected when the Reform Act of 1867 enfranchised workingmen in cities and towns. Only in 1884 was the political power
of the landed classes broken in the countryside by the enfranchise-
ment of agricultural laborers (their votes protected by the ballot)
and by the shift to single-member constituencies in the Redis-
tribution Act of 1885; by then the old "politics of deference" was
coming very close to its end.

Historiographically, this reinterpretation of the Victorian constitution owes much to Sir Lewis Namier's pioneering studies of
mid-eighteenth century politics—*The Structure of Politics at the
Accession of George III* (1929) and *England in the Age of the
American Revolution* (1930)—and to G. Kitson Clark's *Peel and
the Conservative Party* (1929). Since then historians have paid
close attention to the machinery of politics and to its essential
and persistent base in local interests; the most important recent
books are Norman Gash, *Politics in the Age of Peel* (1953), and
H. J. Hanham, *Elections and Party Management; Politics in the
Time of Disraeli and Gladstone* (1959). Gash, Hanham, and others
recognize, of course, that there was change as well as continuity.
An enlarged electorate needed to be mobilized; consequently, after
1832 rudimentary party organizations began gradually to appear
in the constituencies, coordinated at the center by political clubs
and the work of newly professional party agents. Further enlarge-
ment of the electorate in 1867 led to the formation of the Birmingham "caucus" to organize the local radical vote. That in turn
pointed the way to creating national party organizations. At the
same time, Parliament—faced with an increasing demand for legislation on matters that no one would have thought the government's business in the eighteenth century—had to be brought under firmer control by the executive, through a more rigorous
parliamentary timetable and limitation of debate. Many of the
implications of these changes in the electorate and in the inter-
relations of government and Parliament remain to be worked out,
but for the moment many valuable suggestions can be drawn from
K. B. Smellie, *A Hundred Years of English Government* (1937;
2nd ed., 1950), Norman Gash, *Reaction and Reconstruction in*

English Politics, 1832–1852 (1965), John P. Mackintosh, *The British Cabinet* (1962), and by retrospective application of some of the insights to be found in two works primarily concerned with twentieth-century politics: R. T. McKenzie, *British Political Parties* (1955; rev. ed., 1963), and Samuel H. Beer, *British Politics in the Collectivist Age* (1965).

Our knowledge of English political life has been expanded in two directions that avoid the concentration on Parliament that once characterized all political histories. In one direction, a great deal has been learned about local government. Any study of this subject must start with the monumental multivolume *English Local Government* (1906–1929) by Sidney and Beatrice Webb, which describes the multifarious forms that evolved from medieval practices in the seventeenth, eighteenth, and early nineteenth centuries. Reforms in the nineteenth century converted that medieval heritage into modern administration. Local functions were transferred from irresponsible, self-perpetuating oligarchies to responsible and even democratic bodies, and bureaucratic administration replaced the old, essentially judicial procedures. This crucial transformation is not yet expounded in the detail that the Webbs devoted to describing the old system, but K. B. Smellie's brief sketch, *A History of Local Government* (1946; 3rd ed., 1957), establishes the main guidelines. Meanwhile, so far as town government is concerned, the transformation can be traced through individual instances. Four may be mentioned: Arthur Redford, *The History of Local Government in Manchester* (1939–1940); B. D. White, *A History of the Corporation of Liverpool, 1835–1914* (1951); Conrad Gill and Asa Briggs, *History of Birmingham* (1952); and A. Temple Patterson, *Radical Leicester, A History of Leicester, 1780–1850* (1954). The last book goes beyond the history of local government, to examine the social forces that moved the political machinery, as do the brief essays by Asa Briggs in *Victorian Cities* (1964). But, as these titles indicate, we know most about the provincial towns; London and the rural districts are, historically, largely *terra incognita.*

In another direction there has been a burgeoning of administrative history, hardly surprising in a century in which state intervention has come to seem a normal, if sometimes uncomfortable, expectation. The three volumes dealing with the poor law in the Webbs' *English Local Government* are essential, as they bring the story of the poor law (unlike other aspects of local government) down to 1929. Relief of the poor was the most extensive and important social service rendered by the state during the nineteenth century, and many of the procedures worked out in reforming its administration, in 1834 and after, were adapted to other administrative purposes. Of particular interest is a device provided for in the "New Poor Law" of 1834: the central administrative commission. Local authorities were subordinated to it, and a corps of inspectors was established to see that central directives were carried out. Two biographies of early and mid-Victorian civil servants —S. E. Finer, *The Life and Times of Sir Edwin Chadwick* (1952), and R. S. Lambert, *Sir John Simon and English Social Administration* (1963)—are highly relevant to the study of poor law and sanitary reforms and, it is to be hoped, will point the way toward other biographical studies of equal scope and power. There is, curiously, no really satisfactory history of the civil service itself. E. W. Cohen's *The Growth of the British Civil Service, 1780–1939* (1941) is a mere sketch, and the centenary in 1954 of the Trevelyan-Northcote report, which embodied the main ideas of the modern civil service, was barren of historical results. But Lucy Brown, in *The Board of Trade and the Free-Trade Movement* (1958), shows how officials at the Board of Trade used every weapon at their command to bring about a change of policy that would enact the particular theoretical position to which they were so fully committed; and in an important interpretative article, " 'Statesmen in Disguise': Reflexions on the History of the Neutrality of the Civil Service," *Historical Journal*, II (1959), G. Kitson Clark demonstrates from many examples how far early Victorian civil servants were from the presumably nonpartisan and anonymous experts who compose the civil service today.

The important question of the structure of ideas that lay behind Victorian administration is the subject of an important debate over the role of Jeremy Bentham and "Benthamism" in shaping the interventionist state as the Victorians, often unsuspectingly, built it. Finer's life of Chadwick is germane here, because Chadwick was close to Bentham and had worked with him in elaborating a model for a collectivist, bureaucratic state. The argument that Benthamism was crucial in expanding state intervention is advanced in two articles: J. B. Brebner, "Laissez-faire and State Intervention in Nineteenth-Century Britain," *Journal of Economic History, Supplement,* VIII (1948), and Henry Parris, "The Nineteenth-Century Revolution in Government: A Reappraisal Reappraised," *Historical Journal,* III (1960). But Parris is replying to a powerful argument that administrative developments arose from autonomous pressures inherent in the administrative process itself, an argument to be found in Oliver MacDonagh, "The Nineteenth-Century Revolution in Government: A Reappraisal," *Historical Journal,* I (1958), and worked out in a particular instance in his study of the regulation of emigrant passenger traffic, *A Pattern of Government Growth, 1800–1860* (1961). The issue has not been resolved and can only be brought closer to solution by many more studies of particular departments and administrators, studies that must not rest content with invoking systems of ideas but that must painstakingly analyze the intellectual obligations of the men involved.

The Substance of Politics

Natural though the resort to state intervention seems to modern minds, to most Victorians it was a last resort. The inefficient, corrupt, and expensive machinery of the eighteenth-century state had with great effort and imagination been swept away or reformed, a process begun, as W. R. Brock has made clear in *Lord Liverpool and Liberal Toryism, 1820 to 1827* (1941), well before 1832 in response to a growing realization of the imperatives of administration. Once the course toward freedom was set, and as long as memories of the old system remained, it was not easy to accept a new appeal to a state: the new state might very well turn out to be like the old one. To some of the most radical minds, the nineteenth century seemed to offer the first chance in human history to try the spontaneous operation of enlightened freedom, and if the state had to be called in to create either enlightenment or freedom, it was only a temporary device to speed the coming of the new order, when coercion would no longer be needed.

Strengthened by moral certainty and a strong religious impulse, this faith in freedom stimulated the greatest crusade of the century for a step in social policy—the repeal of the corn laws, those tariffs on imported grain that served so poorly as protection for the agricultural interests of the country and so well as an affirmation of the traditional importance of landed society. As Norman McCord amply demonstrates in *The Anti-Corn Law League, 1838–1846* (1958), the League was not the major factor in bringing about repeal in 1846; that was done by the pragmatic conversion of Peel and enough parliamentary supporters. But the League, a political weapon of seemingly unlimited power, created a faith in free trade that half a century later could defeat proposals to return to protection. In R. T. Shannon's *Gladstone and the Bulgarian Agitation, 1876* (1963), another crusade is superbly documented, this time in the area of foreign affairs. Like the corn law campaign, the Bulgarian agitation illustrates the persistent moral strain in English liberalism. To understand that emphasis on moral imperatives helps to explain the dominating part played for nearly half a century by W. E. Gladstone, a statesman whose religious dedication and cloudy rhetoric largely elude the sympathies of our own century.

The radicals' confidence in human nature was not entirely misplaced. For at least a century before 1815 there had been a steady growth of humanitarian feeling and voluntary charitable activity; it could easily seem that if these impulses were generalized and made more intelligent and discriminating, all social problems could be solved. Much remains to be learned about this alternative route for social policy. Missionary enterprise overseas, certainly one of philanthropy's most important outlets, has been consistently ignored by historians, with the notable exception of Owen Chadwick's *Mackenzie's Grave* (1959). Chadwick's moving account of the first Anglican bishopric in central Africa reveals not only the zeal that could lead men to martyrdom but the terrible moral conflicts encountered in trying to impose the standards of one civilization upon another. Philanthropy is much better served at home. In the chapters dealing with the nineteenth century, David Owen's *English Philanthropy, 1660–1960* (1964), charts the crucial transformations in the impulses and forms of charity, while noting its increasing institutionalization and the conservatively helpful attitude of the state in making the application of charity more intelligent and effective. The book is also a guide to the scholarship of the subject. Two biographies may, however, be singled out for mention here: T. S. and Margaret Simey's *Charles Booth, Social Scientist* (1960) and Asa Briggs's *Social Thought and Social Action: A Study of the Work of Seebohm Rowntree, 1871–1954* (1961). The lives of these two social investigators illustrate the continuing strength of individual moral concern for social reform and its deep roots in religion and local culture.

It became increasingly clear as the century progressed that the ultimate solution to social problems lay, not in philanthropy or reformed human nature, but with the state. At no time before the twentieth century, however, did questions of social policy dominate politics. By the end of the nineteenth century, to be sure, there were signs among wealthier and more conservative Englishmen that they did not like the drift of state policy. But no government fell on such a question. Nineteenth-century politics turned on traditional issues; besides the constitutional questions such as parliamentary reform, they included foreign affairs, the relations between church and state, and Ireland.

R. W. Seton-Watson's *Britain in Europe, 1789–1914* (1937) is a useful sketch of diplomatic history; and there are three monumental studies of great foreign secretaries: H. W. V. Temperley, *The Foreign Policy of Canning, 1822–1827* (1925); and C. K. Webster, *The Foreign Policy of Castlereagh* (1925 and 1931) and *The Foreign Policy of Palmerston, 1830–1841* (1951). These volumes trace the creation of Britain's isolationist and liberal stance (combined in its creators with conservatism at home) during the first half of the nineteenth century. But most recent works in diplomatic history seem confined largely to detailed studies of single incidents or problems and make no contribution to a general reinterpretation of foreign policy. The notable exception is *Africa and the Victorians* (1961) by Ronald Robinson and John Gallagher; while it may belong primarily to the category of imperial studies excluded from this essay, it is a brilliant interpretation of Britain's place in a European diplomacy that had changed out of all recognition. Late Victorian Britain no longer had the initiative. Rather she responded with traditional pragmatism to Continental competition inflamed by her clumsy and largely unintended occupation of Egypt in 1882. By the end of the nineteenth century Britain was at war in South Africa, isolated by the choice of others, not her own. The way out of isolation—into Empire, the American "alliance," and the realigned diplomacy of Europe—can still be best followed in Halévy's epilogue. The interaction of foreign and domestic politics, Shannon's admirable study aside, has not been dealt with seriously.

In ecclesiastical policy, nineteenth-century statesmen were faced with a nation divided (leaving aside the large numbers of the apathetic who were so disturbing to religious men) into adherents of the Established Church and the Dissenters. In the eighteenth century the Dissenters were, if not satisfied, at least generally uncomplaining about the legal discriminations against them, reinforced by often more galling and certainly longer-lasting social discrimination. Slowly, piecemeal, those legal discriminations were lifted. In 1828 Dissenters became eligible to hold public office without subterfuge or connivance; they were gradually freed from the necessity of contributing financial support to the Establishment; after 1836 they could be married in their own chapels; from the mid-'fifties they could attend both Oxford and Cambridge and take degrees; after 1871 they could hold any university office or fellowship. These concessions were in part responses to a growing liberalism or a growing religious indifference. Less than they might seem were they responses to political pressure, for not until the last half of the century did Dissenters become a formidable political bloc. Even then they never approached the strength necessary to carry the disestablishment of the Anglican Church, which became the main political goal for so many Dissenters by mid-century.

Victorian statesmen were faced as well with a Church divided. The Oxford Movement of the 1830's, with its emphasis on the visible Church and Catholic tradition and with its implied threat (made the more terrible by some important conversions) of a return to Rome, transformed the Church at the same time that it exasperated most laymen and politicians. Ranged solidly against the Oxford Movement or the Tractarians, as its adherents were often called, and against their successors in the later ritualistic

High Church movement were the Evangelicals. Evangelicals, at least in their earlier generations, proclaimed a religion of conversion, a direct experience of God's grace, which led them to play down the visible Church and the ecclesiastical tradition so important to high Churchmen. The Evangelical impulse could run to social reform, such as antislavery or factory legislation, or to moral reform, such as temperance and Sabbatarianism; it could be welcome or embarrassing to politicians as their own inclinations or tactical necessities might indicate. But Evangelicalism, particularly in the latter part of the century, could also lead to an obscurantism or a brute anti-Catholicism that was as difficult to deal with as it was unedifying. Both High and Low Church resisted what they called liberalism. Yet liberalism grew steadily, responding to the new imperatives of scientific fact and theory and to the "higher criticism" that did so much to undermine the authority of the Bible and to invalidate the axioms that had dominated intellectual life for more than a thousand years.

In this treacherous situation, English statesmen had to try to reform the Church of England, to make it more responsive to a complex society in which its claims were no longer so freely recognized. The administrative history of the nineteenth-century Church, which revolves around the creation of the Ecclesiastical Commission in 1836, is the subject of G. F. A. Best's magisterial *Temporal Pillars* (1964). The successive conflicts of church and state over issues of principle, in which the state seemed invariably to emerge the victor, are delightfully sketched in A. O. J. Cockshut, *Anglican Attitudes* (1959); the paradoxical conclusion is advanced, quite correctly, that in actuality the Church was allowed to go pretty much its own way, however contrary that way was to decisions of legally constituted secular authority. Finally, it should be said that for the period down to 1860, there is an imposing and authoritative guide to Anglican history in Owen Chadwick, *The Victorian Church* (1966).

Probably the most pervasive religious controversy in nineteenth-century politics revolved around education: few men could conceive of secular education, and not many were willing to sacrifice their sectarian vested interests to the monopoly of one sect or to a nondenominational compromise. But no very great advances have been made in writing the history of nineteenth-century education, either at the level of the universities, the secondary schools, or the primary schools for the working classes; J. R. Murphy's *The Religious Problem in English Education: The Crucial Experiment* (1959) does, however, illustrate in the case of Liverpool how deeply religious passions entered into and bedeviled improvement in this vital area of social policy.

Ireland has probably been the best served by historians of any of the major, traditional political problems, a fitting state of things since Ireland was the most persistent and disruptive of those problems. In part, the Irish problem was religious, for Ireland was a Catholic country with a large Protestant minority in the northern province of Ulster, which was itself to become a source of difficulty at the end of the nineteenth century. The Irish problem was also economic, for Ireland had a far larger population than it could support and tried to maintain that population by a wasteful and inefficient system of agriculture so closely tied in with English landed interests that any change was difficult to imagine, let alone implement. Governing Ireland from England had never worked well, and English failures led to one after another political challenge, first in Daniel O'Connell's demand for "Catholic Emancipation" (the right of Catholics to hold office and to sit in Parliament), then in his demand for repeal of the Union, and ultimately in the demand, with Charles Stewart Parnell as its greatest spokesman, for "home rule."

During most of the first half of the century Englishmen tried to solve Irish problems by making Ireland English, by trying to convert her agriculture to the English pattern of large, heavily capitalized estates, or even by making Ireland Protestant. During the last half of the century, more and more concessions to a Catholic and peasant reality were painfully made. These steps brought bitter resistance from Ulster and from Conservative and imperialist Englishmen; Gladstone's abortive attempt in 1886 to bring about home rule split the Liberal Party. For all the success of later schemes for land purchase and "killing Home Rule by kindness," an appreciation of Irish nationalism remained beyond the grasp of most Englishmen, and in 1914 the two countries were on the verge of civil war. This pamphlet cannot do justice to Irish history, even in its own period, but because Ireland was so vital to English politics, the leading recent studies must be noted: R. B. McDowell, *Public Opinion and Government Policy in Ireland, 1801–1846* (1952); Angus Macintyre, *The Liberator: Daniel O'Connell and the Irish Party, 1830–1847* (1965); Conor Cruise O'Brien, *Parnell and his Party 1880–90* (1957), a brilliant demonstration of how an essentially moderate policy was supported by extremist tactics; F. S. L. Lyons, *The Fall of Parnell, 1890–91* (1960) and *The Irish Parliamentary Party, 1890–1910* (1951); and L. P. Curtis, Jr., *Coercion and Conciliation in Ireland, 1880–1892* (1963). The watershed in nineteenth-century Irish history was the famine of 1845–1847. This disaster reduced the population of Ireland, by death and emigration, by some two millions and left a legacy of bitterness and guilt that made relations between the two countries infinitely worse than they had been in the occasionally hopeful days of the 1830's. The fullest narrative account is Cecil Woodham-Smith, *The Great Hunger* (1962), but its passionate indictment of English policy should be read in conjunction with the dispassionate and authoritative essays in R. Dudley Edwards and T. Desmond Williams, eds., *The Great Famine* (1957).

This survey of the machinery and the substance of parliamentary politics in the nineteenth century should have demonstrated how far, with certain notable gaps, historical knowledge has grown in extent and sophistication in recent years. It is depressing to have to report that, by contrast, political biography has made very little progress. Sir Philip Magnus's portrait in *Gladstone, a Biography* (1954) is a fine exception to this generalization, and by their sweep and size Norman Gash's *Mr. Secretary Peel* (1961), so far brought down only to 1830, and Robert Blake's *Disraeli* (1966), though traditional in form, promise to do nearly all one could wish for two of the greatest of Victorian prime ministers. But many of the most important political figures are without serious modern assessments. Biographies written in recent years have varied somewhat in their competence and almost not at all in their readability, but they remain firmly fixed in an old, narrowly political narrative tradition. They give far too little attention, on the one hand, to the psychological and intellectual wellsprings of their subjects' actions and, on the other hand, to the institutional context and challenges that these men can illuminate and that in turn may help to explain their dilemmas and imperatives.

The Transformation of English Society

The brute fact to which Sir Lewis Namier drew historians' attention a generation ago is that politics is about interests. The politically meaningful interests with which Sir Lewis Namier dealt in his studies of the 1760's were confined to factions and connections within a small but all-important segment of society— the landed classes and a few allies from commerce—who monopolized political power at the center. A century later the clash of interests had grown wider, had indeed been modified out of all recognition. There were signs, even in the mid-eighteenth century, that new segments of what can be called public opinion were stirring, and the late eighteenth century saw one after another hitherto reticent, satisfied, or apathetic element in society turn dissatisfied and vocal. To some extent the challenge to the narrow political oligarchy grew from economic circumstances: from prosperity, as among the newly confident commercial and manufacturing elements in society who were beginning to call themselves the "middle classes"; or from adversity, as with those groups in society to whom the economic revolutions had brought new and unaccustomed disciplines and a changed standard of life. Still another stimulus to the expansion of the field of politics came from the French Revolution, both from its direct challenge to English institutions and from the long war that followed it. This complex of events forced the polarization of eighteenth-century political connections into the nineteenth-century party divisions of Whig and Tory, and it provided ideas, encouragement, and rhetoric for nineteenth-century radicalism, in both its middle-class and working-class embodiments.

These impulses to change issued in the early Victorian period in what Marx and Engels, along with most Englishmen, saw as a class struggle. It was, however, a class struggle in which there was much blurring of class lines. Persistent older forms of social and industrial organization defied ready classification into "bourgeois" and "proletarian," terms of doubtful applicability to England. Social mobility was facilitated by the spread of industrialism; private philanthropy and state intervention helped to soften the worst or most apparent consequences of urban and industrial civilization. To some extent, after 1860 these mitigating factors grew less important, and politics became more clearly concerned with interests than it had been early in Victoria's reign. One need only cite the steady desertion of satisfied industrial and commercial men from the Liberal to the Conservative Party, the rise of a specifically labor party, and the increasingly hysterical resistance of those whose accustomed right to rule was threatened by democracy, a resistance that culminated in the House of Lords crisis of 1909-1911 and the desperate "Tory revolt" of 1911-1914.

This vast transformation of the social realities underlying politics has been illuminated considerably by recent work. G. Kitson Clark's *The Making of Victorian England* (1962) and W. L. Burn's *The Age of Equipoise* (1964) both deal, in their differing ways, with the mid-Victorian generation from about 1850 to 1873. Clark is concerned with the genesis of what might be called High Victorianism, but what he has to say about the political reflection of the old and new forms of upper-class life is highly relevant to this transformation. Professor Burn's amusing, learned, and idiosyncratic book emphasizes the elements of order that made tolerable the liberal theory of mid-century, particularly the forms of law and administration, the disciplines of social deference, and the family. In a very real sense, the landed classes still formed the backbone of society for most of the century. A careful and imaginative account of the economic basis, the social forms, and the assumptions of these key elements is F. M. L. Thompson's *English Landed Society in the Nineteenth Century* (1963), the last chapters of which chronicle and explain the decline of landed power, which determined so much of the political and social tension at the end of the period.

The middle classes are less easy to isolate and analyze. Many of the currents of social and intellectual thought and many economic developments are relevant to an understanding of middle-class England: English culture in the nineteenth century was essentially a middle-class culture. Yet, in many areas that are central to a definition of the middle classes, we must remain content with conjectures in place of solid historical exposition. W. J. Reader's *Professional Men* (1966), however, admirably describes the development of professionalism, one of the two or three main forces that defined and extended the range of the upper middle classes. Understandably his principal emphasis rests on the older, learned professions—medicine, law, and the church—which were transformed in the course of the century by a new discipline in training and a marked rise in social status; from this traditional core, the modes of thought and expectation spread to other, newer professions like engineering and accounting. Reader also draws attention to the spiritual alliance forged between these newly self-conscious, autonomous professionals and traditional English society, with a resulting timidity that prevented the professions from assuming the intellectual and social lead in bringing about fundamental changes. In a similar vein, Noel Annan's article, "The Intellectual Aristocracy," in J. H. Plumb, ed., *Studies in Social History: A Tribute to G. M. Trevelyan* (1955), provides a guide to understanding the phenomenon of a Victorian intelligentsia that resulted from grafting an old clerical and university tradition onto newly prominent industrial and commercial families. Thanks to intermarriage, effective recruitment, and an extraordinarily high level of accomplishment and social responsibility, the intellectual aristocracy became and has remained a vital force in English life. It has accepted modified forms of traditional aristocratic values and has been, in contrast to the situation in some other countries, allied with the main political forces in the nation, not alienated from them.

These two valuable general discussions pose the problems with which any discussion of separate professions must deal. There are useful histories of less exalted professions in A. Tropp's *The School Teachers* (1957) and Brian Abel-Smith's *A History of the Nursing Profession* (1960). But medicine, probably the key profession of the century, needs much intensive work. For the practice of law there is no nineteenth-century successor to Robert Robson's informative study of *The Attorney in Eighteenth-Century England* (1959), and we know little about the creative Victorian judges, except for the wealth of suggestion in C. H. S. Fifoot's brief lectures, *Judge and Jurist in the Reign of Victoria*

(1959). On the clergy, Diana McClatchey, *Oxfordshire Clergy, 1777–1869* (1960), is admirably detailed but insufficiently generalized. The profession of university teaching emerges in an entirely new, and truly professional, form after the abolition of the last religious tests in 1870. Like most university history of the period, university teaching remains unstudied, a few useful memoirs aside.

Another area essential to an understanding of the middle classes is the spread of moral ideas from the middle classes up and down the social scale. Largely ignorant of Victorian sexual practices and theories, we are better served in regard to the family and the position of women, who were on their way after mid-century toward "emancipation" not only in politics but from the ties of household routine and from the isolation and futility of that idealization which was so stern a guarantee of the permanence of the family and the security of respectability. Working-class women had, of course, long gone out to work; and while little is known about Victorian servants, there is a fair amount of information about the conditions of female factory labor. But very little has been written about the gradual realization of the potential of middle-class women, although some of its preconditions have been dealt with. O. R. McGregor's *Divorce in England* (1957) contains an admirable chapter on the Victorian family as well as an account of the legal emancipation of women and particularly the provision of legal remedies against husbands to whom, before 1857, married women had been completely subordinated. J. A. Banks, *Prosperity and Parenthood* (1954), offers an ingenious hypothesis, based on the rising cost of living, for the marked decline in middle-class family size late in the century, a study from which much fascinating incidental information can be drawn about the patterns of middle-class life. On any question dealing with women, O. R. McGregor's bibliography, "The Social Position of Women in England, 1850–1914," *British Journal of Sociology,* VI (1955), is essential.

Historical knowledge is much more extensive, at least in quantity, so far as the working classes are concerned. There are signs, too, that working-class history is beginning to break the bonds of political and sentimental commitment that have held most of its practitioners, or, at any rate, that those commitments are ceasing to be read automatically into working-class history as facts and are becoming critical tools instead. The central book, sweeping through the period from the 1790's to 1830, is E. P. Thompson's *The Making of the English Working Class* (1963). When Thompson has his passions under control (as he does not always), he contributes impressively to an understanding of the cultural and social factors that led English workingmen to think of themselves as a class.

On the political side, the history of working-class movements after 1832 falls into three periods. In the Chartist period, the old London-centered views have been drastically altered by studies of individual Chartists and of Chartism as it was manifested in different parts of the country: G. D. H. Cole, *Chartist Portraits* (1941); A. Schoyen, *The Chartist Challenge* (1958), a life of the left-wing leader G. J. Harney; Asa Briggs, ed., *Chartist Studies* (1959); and David Williams, *John Frost* (1939) and *The Rebecca Riots* (1955), the former a study of Welsh Chartism as it culminated in the one Chartist rising (at Newport in 1839), the latter a brilliant study of rural violence in the 1840's and, beyond that, an investigation of the decay of Welsh rural society. There is as yet no general history of Chartism to take advantage of these studies, but if ever it is written, it will show a phenomenon of the greatest complexity in impulse and motivation and with results as ambiguous as the conflicting ambitions poured into the vessel of the narrowly political six points of the Charter. Mid-Victorian working-class history has long been well served by Frances Gillespie, *Labor and Politics in England, 1850–1867* (1927), but now much extremely valuable information on the background of the 1867 reform act is to be found in Royden Harrison, *Before the Socialists* (1965). In this period the volcanic activity of the Chartist generation cooled down into solid organization, particularly on the trade-union side. From that base it was possible for the leaders of mid-Victorian labor— called the "Junta" by Sidney and Beatrice Webb—to move not only to secure a firm legal base for trade-union activity but to begin a successful assertion of working-class political claims by getting the vote for workingmen and by winning seats for working-class representatives in the House of Commons. The third period is characterized by the gradual diversion of labor politics from the mere avowal and defense of class interests, usually in association with the Liberal Party, to independent political action as a Labor Party. The beginning of this political shift is clearly delineated in Henry Pelling, *The Origins of the Labour Party, 1880–1900* (1954). But working-class movements in the nineteenth-century were not merely political; they were trade-unionist and socialist as well.

Sidney and Beatrice Webb's *The History of Trade Unionism* (1894; rev. ed., 1920) now creaks badly. An encyclopedic *History of British Trade Unions since 1889*, by H. A. Clegg, Alan Fox, and A. F. Thompson, has begun to appear; but the first volume (1964), which carries the story down to 1911, amasses vast amounts of information without offering any clear interpretative structure. A few monographs aside, only E. H. Phelps Brown, *The Growth of British Industrial Relations* (1959), breaks new ground. In studying the labor problem during 1906–1914, when strikes were so frequent and alarming, Professor Brown surveys the development of the forms and assumptions of trade unionism throughout the nineteenth century. He is particularly revealing in his attention to the emergence of grievances which resulted from the changing nature of work; he also disinters those forms of industrial organization, like arbitration, that for a time in the late nineteenth century seemed to be possible alternative ways of organizing industrial relations. But, after a period of experimentation, the older device of collective bargaining was confirmed as the principal means of negotiation between capital and labor.

The history of socialism is similarly riddled with gaps: there are, for example, no recent or really satisfactory assessments of Robert Owen and Owenism, that "utopian socialist" movement from which so much English socialism descended. Nor are there any good studies of cooperation, other than Torben Christensen's admirable *Origins and History of Christian Socialism, 1848–54* (1962), or of the British role in the international socialist movement. A. M. McBriar makes an important critical advance, however, in his *Fabian Socialism and English Politics, 1884–1918* (1962). After an account of the origins of the Fabian Society and a careful exposition of its wide-ranging and complex attitudes, he suggests that its role in affecting policy through "permeation" was not so great as Fabian historians would have it.

The decline of the landed classes and the assertive claims of labor posed a new dilemma for the middle classes: whether to move toward a new radicalism or to identify themselves with the old order and reassert those characteristics that Beatrice Webb had noted in her own family, the habit of giving orders and being obeyed. The older attitude was powerful and attractive, especially when the exercise of power was humanized by a sense of honor and obligation, so sedulously implanted in the schools where the sons of the well-to-do were educated. A. P. Thornton has given an exemplary analysis of these assumptions in *The Habit of Authority* (1966). But a new radicalism, or a new liberalism, developed, too; it was proto-socialist or at any rate no longer distrustful of the state, susceptible to Continental, particularly German, examples, and infused with ideals of social service and belief in a positive, organic society. The roots of this new departure were various. One strain descended from the teaching of the Oxford idealists, the most influential of whom was T. H. Green. Green's curious blend of secularized Evangelical religion and Hegelianism has been admirably analyzed by Melvin Richter in *The Politics of Conscience* (1964). Another strain came from radical Nonconformity, for which, at least in its Welsh manifestation, David Lloyd George was the principal spokesman. Still another found its roots in the democratic politics of provincial towns, where so much had been done after mid-century in housing reform and municipal ownership of public utilities; the main political beneficiary of this tradition was Joseph Chamberlain. But when Chamberlain's radicalism and ambition were frustrated in the Liberal Party, and when he found himself unable to accept Home Rule as a solution to the Irish problem, he moved over to the Conservatives. There he turned to schemes for imperial unity and, in time, imperial protective tariffs. The change is an important reminder that, in many of its adherents, the new radicalism was closely linked to imperialism in an amalgam of ideas which are analyzed by Bernard Semmel in *Imperialism and Social Reform* (1960). Still, the new liberalism did not carry with it a majority of the descendants of the partisans of Cobden and Bright half a century earlier; they found their way into Conservatism.

The Liberal governments in 1905–1914 presented the problems of liberalism in a particularly acute form. It was a time of astonishingly creative social legislation, but it was also a time of extreme tensions—the Tory rebellion over Ireland, the extensive strikes and semi-syndicalist pressure of the trade unions, and the hysterical violence of the suffragette campaign; the terrible years of 1911–1914 mark the end of Victorian England. Some amusing and able popular books have appeared on the Edwardian Age, but serious historical exploration has barely begun. Other than Halévy's epilogue, the most readable and suggestive account of the whole period is still George Dangerfield's scintillating *The Strange Death of Liberal England* (1935).

The Spread of Industrialism

England was the first industrial society. In the first three-quarters of the nineteenth century, it was subjected to stresses unexampled before and unequalled since. The very newness of the experience meant that there were no lessons to be learned, as other countries were able to learn from England. Moreover, nearly all of the financing of this transformation came from England; only Soviet Russia in the twentieth century has faced a comparable challenge of industrializing without substantial investment from abroad. These facts help to explain the bleak appearance of much social history down to 1850. They are less important factors in the suffering of the time, however, than the rapid growth of population, the inadequacy of town resources, the reorientation of the economic map, and the breaking of successive generations of workers to the discipline and speed of industrial labor. But terrible as they were in many respects, the first five decades of the century were also the time when the foundations of England's prosperity were laid: her human and material resources were harnessed, a vast stock of capital was created, and England came to dominate an empire and a world that wanted what only England had to sell. In the quarter-century between the failure of the last Chartist demonstration in 1848 and 1873, England was at the peak of her power; the relative social and political calm of the 'fifties is testimony to the expansiveness that came with her escape into prosperity. But after 1873, the rest of the western world began to catch up and, in many respects, to surpass England. By 1896, England no longer had her monopoly, and many contemporaries felt that the years between were in fact what historians have called them—"the great depression." The return of boom times between 1896 and 1914 only masked a relative decline that, seen from the vantage point of the 1960's, bordered on the disastrous.

This four-fold division of the century after Waterloo is inescapable, but in recent years our knowledge of the forces that shaped each of these periods has grown in complexity and sophistication. This advance has benefited greatly from the shifting concerns and conceptions of economic theorists; to cite but one example, some highly fruitful inquiries into the history of English industrialism have grown out of economists' thinking about the problem of development in backward countries today. Where only a few book titles can be mentioned, little justice can be done to the range of present-day knowledge of the Victorian economy, particularly since so much of the contribution has been made in articles. Hence this discussion must begin with mention of four recent books that not only summarize the present state of scholarship for their respective periods but serve admirably as guides to that scholarship: Phyllis Deane, *The First Industrial Revolution* (1965); S. G. Checkland, *The Rise of Industrial Society in England, 1815–1885* (1964); William Ashworth, *An Economic History of England, 1870–1939* (1961); and W. H. B. Court, *British Economic History, 1870–1914: Commentary and Documents* (1965).

No serious student can dispense with Sir John Clapham's massive *An Economic History of Modern Britain* (1927–1938), the three volumes of which cover the period from 1830 to 1914; its scope and detail make evident how complex the Victorian economy was, how far it represented a mixture of innovation and survival. In doing so, Clapham made forever impossible the confident simplicities in which economic history had too often been understood before he wrote. In his powerful attack on the pessimistic conclusions of J. L. and Barbara Hammond about the effects of industrialism on living standards among the poor, Clapham initiated a debate that in recent years has been taken up again with new liveliness. It may be asked whether the debate can ever be conclusive, for efforts at convincing statistical measurement seem destined to perpetual defeat, and more impressionistic efforts depend so much on the period, region, industry, or even individuals chosen. Some people prospered, particularly those in new and highly skilled lines of work created by industrialism; others suffered desperately, particularly those in trades, like handloom weaving, that were doomed by technological advance. For most people, perhaps, the way of life changed, and change (at least until one becomes accustomed to it) may be difficult; but this adjustment must be weighed in turn against the raised levels of expectation and increased opportunities that came with greater mobility. Most of the time, the historian's position in the end rests on his political and social predilections. But this debate over the standard of living is confined to the first half of the century. From 1850 to 1896, there was not only a fall in prices (that had been going on throughout the century) but a marked and general rise in real wages—i.e., in the amount of goods that could be bought with a given sum in wages—and a wide diffusion of prosperity among the working classes. The "great depression" was by and large a golden age for labor, a generalization not undone by pointing to the poverty that still remained, as it remains even today. In the early years of the twentieth century, however, this improvement was not maintained: the rise in prices outstripped the rise in wages and contributed to the tensions of the prewar decade.

Standard of living aside, historians have turned away from the concerns that dominate Clapman's volumes. His interests, and the main value of the book, lay in his accounts of technology and the institutions and structure of the economy; the descriptive function overweighs analytical and dynamic questions. Such questions were raised in a highly stimulating way, at about the time Clapham was finishing his *History,* by W. W. Rostow; *The British Economy of the Nineteenth Century,* published in 1948, consists of articles published over the preceding dozen years. Rostow's inquiries were necessarily fragmentary, tentative proposals rather than firm and sweeping conclusions, but it is testimony to his forcefulness that the book is still an important point of departure. More far-reaching and now likely to be the book from which the advances of the next few decades must begin is Phyllis Deane and W. A. Cole, *British Economic Growth, 1688–1959* (1962). Here the emphasis, while not neglecting institutional and structural change in the economy, is on such long-term dynamic factors as population growth, migration, the patterns of international trade, the formation of capital, and the composition and growth of national income.

The debates among demographers may always be most interesting for the period when statistical information was least reliable, before the first census was taken in 1801. But the steady growth of population throughout the nineteenth century and the changing distribution of that population, thanks to factors like changing family size or emigration, had economic consequences of great magnitude. Very little can be said confidently about conclusions from the debate about population, and it is perhaps best dealt with here by referring to *Population in History,* ed. D. V. Glass and D. E. C. Eversley (1965), in which the principal articles are collected.

One can speak much more confidently about the formation of capital and its employment. The enormous enterprise of railway-building dominated the fifty years after 1830. Railways were important not only because they revolutionized patterns of life and business but because their demands contributed directly or indirectly to the prosperity of much of the country's industry. Rostow, as a matter of fact, explains the "great depression"—which we have long known was no real depression but rather a crisis of confidence among some businessmen, brought on by falling profit margins—as a natural consequence of the passing of the boom years of early industrialism: it was bound to happen once the railways were built. But Charles Wilson, in "Economy and Society in Late Victorian Britain," *Economic History Review,* XVIII (1965), argues that this "depression" was confined to those older staple industries that had dominated the period of the "industrial revolution" and on which Britain was dependent to a dangerous degree. In this same period, however, there was heavy investment—and a good rate of profit—in new industries, chemicals for example, and in the new and rapidly expanding modern forms of the retail trade, such as department stores and chain stores. These "new sectors" of the domestic economy, not to mention overseas enterprises, did not suffer from what Clapham called "the chill and heavy air of Lombard Street," and were not lacking, as were many older industries, in managerial skills. A similar diversification was under way in agriculture, where the traditional main crops like wheat were hard hit by foreign competition after 1873; but dairying and specialty farming prospered, thanks to a rising standard of living. The classic history of English agriculture, Lord Ernle's *English Farming, Past and Present* (1912), can now be used for the nineteenth century only if read in conjunction with the introduction to the most recent edition by G. E. Fussell and O. R. McGregor (1962) and T. W. Fletcher's revisionist article, "The Great Depression in English Agriculture, 1873-1896," *Economic History Review*, XIII (1961).

Britain had early become dependent on her export trade; that export trade was in turn dependent on a few industries, industries that other countries could easily establish and often operate more efficiently. As her export trade declined in its older markets, England had to face stiffer competition not only there but in new markets. At the same time, as her prosperity increased, her bill for imports rose. The country had an unfavorable balance of trade throughout the century, a conclusion that has been ingeniously disentangled from a welter of statistics by A. H. Imlah in his *Economic Factors in the Pax Britannica* (1958). How was it that she was able to survive a chronic imbalance? Increasingly throughout the century England relied for her prosperity on her "invisible exports," those services—shipping, banking, insurance—that she could perform better than anyone else in the world and on the income from investments overseas. The earlier history of overseas investment has been dealt with in a long-standard and delightful study by L. H. Jenks, *The Migration of British Capital to 1875* (1927), a story of successive and not always successful efforts by investors to find large returns in South America, the United States, and continental Europe. But in the forty years after 1870 British investment overseas grew from a modest supplement to a major support of the economy. A. K. Cairncross estimates in *Home and Foreign Investment, 1870-1913* (1953), the authoritative book on the subject, that in order to equal annual British investments overseas in 1913, Americans in 1951 would have had to invest abroad twenty times as much as they did, the equivalent of the Marshall Plan twice over every year. The "prosperity" of prewar England was hardly surprising; and the loss of such "cushions" in the twentieth century goes far toward explaining much of the painful readjustment that the British economy has had to make.

The Victorian Intellect

The field of Victorian intellectual and cultural history is so vast and so unevenly plowed that no attempt can be made here to explore its problems or conclusions in any depth. To note a few guides and a few outstanding books is as much to point to what needs doing as to what has been done well. Literary history has become a discipline with increasingly weaker ties to other kinds of history; large numbers of works of literary criticism are simply beyond mastery by social historians. There are, however, two excellent general books whose bent is literary but which are of the greatest interest and help to historians: Walter E. Houghton, *The Victorian Frame of Mind, 1830-1870* (1957), and J. H. Buckley, *The Victorian Temper* (1951).

Architecture, socially the most important of the arts, flourished in the Victorian generations, and its monuments have come increasingly to be admired in recent years. But after Henry-Russell Hitchcock's imposing *Early Victorian Architecture in Britain* (1954), one must fall back on H. S. Goodhart-Rendel's brief but stimulating *English Architecture since the Regency* (1953) for a guide to middle and late Victorian and Edwardian developments. No such guides exist at all for Victorian painting and music, perhaps because neither field holds much appeal for modern sensibilities.

One grand theme of the nineteenth-century intellect is the steady decline of religion as the key to men's understanding. G. Kitson Clark's *The Making of Victorian England* is an essential starting point for a comprehension of the religious situation in the crucial mid-Victorian generation, and L. E. Elliot-Binns, *English Thought, 1860-1900: The Theological Aspect* (1956), and K. S. Inglis, *Churches and the Working Classes in Victorian England* (1963), deal with two aspects (the former more successful than the latter) of the readjustment that had to be made. Science is the first source to which one usually looks to understand the stimulus to change in the religious scene, and three books point to the ambiguous contribution of early Victorian scientists: Charles C. Gillispie, *Genesis and Geology* (1951), Gertrude Himmelfarb, *Darwin and the Darwinian Revolution* (1959), and L. Pearce Williams, *Michael Faraday, a Biography* (1965). But other concerns were as corrosive—"higher criticism" and textual scholarship, advances in historical and philosophical thought, moral imperatives to which traditional religion often seemed irrelevant, and struggles within the churches themselves that sometimes ended in division and sterility.

This displacement of religion may be seen as part of a still larger transformation, the fragmentation of a culture in which educated men had for centuries shared a common stock of assumptions and a common language. With the growing complexity of the economy and society, with the reform of the universities and their new orientation toward learning and scholarship, with the expanding professions, and with the advance of all forms of knowledge toward more difficult questions and more sophisticated solutions, the sense of a common enterprise grew increasingly difficult to maintain. The "alienation" of the artist was only one, if the most publicized, result. But one writes such generalizations from an impression that they are true, not from any solid base in historical scholarship. In dealing with ideas, even more with the relation of ideas to society, historians of nineteenth-century England have as yet hardly reached the first broad generalizations—like those of the nineteenth-century Whig political historians or of the Hammonds and other early twentieth-century social historians—in the criticism and destruction of which so much of the progress chronicled in this essay has been made. One inevitably comes back to Halévy, one of the most brilliant practitioners of this kind of history. It is ironic that a historian whose work is so much admired set an example that has been all too little followed.

REFERENCES

Included in this list are the titles of the most important books and articles mentioned in this pamphlet, plus a few additional general histories of nineteenth-century England. Asterisks indicate books that are available in paperback editions.

Annan, Noel. "The Intellectual Aristocracy," in J. H. Plumb, ed., *Studies in Social History: A Tribute to G. M. Trevelyan.* London and New York: Longmans, Green, 1955.

Ashworth, William. *An Economic History of England, 1870–1939.* London: Methuen; New York: Barnes and Noble, 1961.

Banks, J. A. *Prosperity and Parenthood*. London: Routledge and Kegan Paul, 1954.

Best, G. F. A. *Temporal Pillars: Queen Anne's Bounty, the Ecclesiastical Commissioners and the Church of England*. Cambridge, England, and New York: Cambridge University Press, 1964.

Blake, Robert. *Disraeli*. London: Eyre and Spottiswoode, 1966.

*Briggs, Asa. *The Age of Improvement, 1782-1867*. London: Longmans, Green; New York: McKay, 1959. (Paperback: Harper Torchbooks.)

*_____, ed. *Chartist Studies*. London: Macmillan; New York: St. Martin's Press, 1959. (Paperback: St. Martin's Press.)

*Buckley, J. H. *The Victorian Temper: A Study in Literary Culture*. Cambridge, Mass.: Harvard University Press, 1951. (Paperback: Vintage.)

*Burn, W. L. *The Age of Equipoise: A Study of the Mid-Victorian Generation*. London: Allen and Unwin; New York: Norton, 1964. (Paperback: Norton.)

Cairncross, A. K. *Home and Foreign Investment, 1870-1913: Studies in Capital Accumulation*. Cambridge, England, and New York: Cambridge University Press, 1953.

Chadwick, Owen. *Mackenzie's Grave*. London: Hodder and Stoughton, 1959.

_____. *The Victorian Church*, Part I. London: A. and C. Black, 1966.

Checkland, S. G. *The Rise of Industrial Society in England, 1815-1885*. London: Longmans, Green; New York: St. Martin's Press, 1964.

Clapham, J. H. *An Economic History of Modern Britain*. 3 vols. Cambridge, England, and New York: Cambridge University Press, 1927-1938; reprinted, 1950-1952.

Cohen, Emmeline W. *The Growth of the British Civil Service, 1780-1939*. London: Allen and Unwin, 1941.

Cole, G. D. H. *Chartist Portraits*. London: Macmillan, 1941; reprinted, London: Macmillan; New York: St. Martin's Press, 1965.

Court, W. H. B. *British Economic History, 1870-1914: Commentary and Documents*. Cambridge, England, and New York: Cambridge University Press, 1965.

*_____. *A Concise Economic History of Great Britain, 1750 to Recent Times*. Cambridge, England, and New York: Cambridge University Press, 1954. (Paperback: Cambridge University Press.)

*Dangerfield, George. *The Strange Death of Liberal England*. London: Constable, 1936. (Paperback: Capricorn.)

*Deane, Phyllis. *The First Industrial Revolution*. Cambridge, England, and New York: Cambridge University Press, 1965. (Paperback: Cambridge University Press.)

_____, and W. A. Cole. *British Economic Growth, 1688-1959*, Cambridge, England, and New York: Cambridge University Press, 1962.

Ensor, R. C. K. *England, 1870-1914*. Oxford: Clarendon Press; New York: Oxford University Press, 1936.

Ernle, Lord. *English Farming, Past and Present*. London: Longmans, Green, 1912. 6th ed., G. E. Fussell and O. R. McGregor, eds. London: Heinemann; Chicago: Quadrangle Books, 1962.

Finer, S. E. *The Life and Times of Sir Edwin Chadwick*. London: Methuen, 1952.

Fletcher, T. W. "The Great Depression in English Agriculture, 1873-1896," *Economic History Review*, 2nd series, XIII (1961), 417-432.

Gash, Norman. *Mr. Secretary Peel: The Life of Sir Robert Peel to 1830*. London: Longmans, Green; Cambridge, Mass.: Harvard University Press, 1961.

_____. *Politics in the Age of Peel: A Study in the Technique of Parliamentary Representation, 1830-1850*. London and New York: Longmans. Green, 1953.

_____. *Reaction and Reconstruction in English Politics. 1832-1852*. Oxford: Clarendon Press; New York: Oxford University Press, 1965.

Gillespie, Frances E. *Labor and Politics in England, 1850-1867.* Durham, N. C.: Duke University Press, 1927.

Glass, D. V., and D. E. C. Eversley, eds. *Population in History.* London: Arnold, 1965; Chicago: Aldine Publishing Co., 1965.

*Halévy, Élie. *The Growth of Philosophic Radicalism.* Paris: 1901-1904. Translated ed.: London and New York: Macmillan, 1928. (Paperback: Beacon.)

*_____. *A History of the English People in the Nineteenth Century.* 6 vols. Paris: 1913-1932. Translated ed.: London: Benn, 1924-1934, with a posthumous volume, 1947. (Paperback: Barnes and Noble.)

Hanham, H. J. *Elections and Party Management; Politics in the Time of Disraeli and Gladstone.* London: Longmans, Green, 1959.

Hitchcock, Henry-Russell. *Early Victorian Architecture in Britain.* 2 vols. New Haven: Yale University Press, 1954.

*Houghton, Walter E. *The Victorian Frame of Mind, 1830-1870.* New Haven: Yale University Press; London: Oxford University Press, 1957. (Paperback: Yale University Press.)

Imlah, A. H. *Economic Factors in the Pax Britannica: Studies in British Foreign Trade in the Nineteenth Century.* Cambridge, Mass.: Harvard University Press, 1958.

Jenks, L. H. *The Migration of British Capital to 1875.* London and New York: Knopf, 1927; reprinted, London and New York: Nelson, 1963.

Kitson Clark, G. *The Making of Victorian England.* London: Methuen; Cambridge, Mass.: Harvard University Press, 1962.

_____. " 'Statesmen in Disguise': Reflexions on the History of the Neutrality of the Civil Service," *Historical Journal,* II (1959), 19-39.

Lambert, Royston. *Sir John Simon, 1816-1904, and English Social Administration.* London: Macgibbon and Kee, 1963.

McBriar, A. M. *Fabian Socialism and English Politics, 1884-1918.* Cambridge, England, and New York: Cambridge University Press, 1962.

McCord, Norman. *The Anti-Corn Law League, 1838-1846.* London: Allen and Unwin, 1958.

MacDonagh, Oliver. "The Nineteenth-Century Revolution in Government: A Reappraisal," *Historical Journal,* I (1958), 52-67.

McGregor, O. R. *Divorce in England, A Centenary Study.* London: Heinemann, 1957.

_____. "The Social Position of Women in England, 1850-1914," *British Journal of Sociology,* VI (1955), 48-60.

*Magnus, Sir Philip. *Gladstone, a Biography.* London: Murray; New York: Dutton, 1964. (Paperback: Dutton.)

O'Brien, Conor Cruise. *Parnell and His Party, 1880-1890.* Oxford: Clarendon Press; New York: Oxford University Press, 1957; 2nd ed., 1964.

Owen, David. *English Philanthropy, 1660-1960.* Cambridge, Mass.: Belknap Press of Harvard University, 1964.

Parris, Henry. "The Nineteenth-Century Revolution in Government: A Reappraisal Reappraised," *Historical Journal,* III (1960), 17-37.

Pelling, Henry. *The Origins of the Labour Party, 1880-1900.* London: Macmillan; New York: St. Martin's Press, 1954; 2nd ed., Oxford: Clarendon Press; New York: Oxford University Press, 1965.

*Phelps Brown, E. H. *The Growth of British Industrial Relations: A Study from the Standpoint of 1906-14.* London: Macmillan; New York: St. Martin's Press, 1959. (Paperback: St. Martin's Press.)

Reader, W. J. *Professional Men.* London: Weidenfeld and Nicolson; New York: Basic Books, Inc., 1967.

Redford, Arthur. *The History of Local Government in Manchester.* 3 vols. London and New York: Longmans, Green, 1939–1940.

Richter, Melvin. *The Politics of Conscience: T. H. Green and his Age.* London: Weidenfeld and Nicolson; Cambridge, Mass.: Harvard University Press, 1964.

Robinson, Ronald, and John Gallagher. *Africa and the Victorians: The Official Mind of Imperialism.* London: Macmillan; New York: St. Martin's Press, 1961.

Rostow, W. W. *The British Economy of the Nineteenth Century.* Oxford: Clarendon Press; New York: Oxford University Press, 1948.

Semmel, Bernard. *Imperialism and Social Reform, English Social-Imperial Thought, 1895–1914.* London: Allen and Unwin; Cambridge, Mass.: Harvard University Press, 1960.

Seton-Watson, R. W. *Britain in Europe, 1789–1914, a Survey of Foreign Policy.* Cambridge, England: Cambridge University Press; New York: Macmillan, 1937; reprinted, 1955.

Shannon, R. T. *Gladstone and the Bulgarian Agitation, 1876.* London and New York: Nelson, 1963.

Smellie, K. B. *A History of Local Government.* London: Allen and Unwin, 1946; 3rd ed., 1957.

———. *A Hundred Years of English Government.* London: Duckworth, 1937; 2nd ed., 1950.

*Thompson, E. P. *The Making of the English Working Class.* London: Gollancz, 1963; New York: Pantheon, 1964. (Paperback: Vintage.)

Thompson, F. M. L. *English Landed Society in the Nineteenth Century.* London: Routledge and Kegan Paul, 1963.

Thornton, A. P. *The Habit of Authority.* London: Allen and Unwin; Toronto: University of Toronto Press, 1966.

Webb, R. K. *A History of Modern England, from the Eighteenth Century to the Present.* New York: Dodd, Mead, 1967.

Webb, Sidney and Beatrice. *English Local Government.* 11 vols. London and New York: Longmans, Green, 1906–1929; reprinted, Hamden, Conn.: Archon, 1963.

Williams, David. *John Frost: A Study in Chartism.* Cardiff: University of Wales Press Board, 1939.

———. *The Rebecca Riots: A Study in Agrarian Discontent.* Cardiff: University of Wales Press Board, 1955.

Wilson, Charles. "Economy and Society in Late Victorian Britain," *Economic History Review,* 2nd series, XVIII (1965), 183–198.

Woodward, E. L. *The Age of Reform, 1815–1870.* Oxford: Clarendon Press; New York: Oxford University Press, 1938, 2nd ed., 1962.

CONFERENCES

FOR

HISTORY TEACHERS

To promote the general objective of maintaining and improving standards of history teaching, the *Service Center* also sponsors conferences for history teachers. These meetings, held in conjunction with the department of history at a college or university or with a state or regional council for the social studies, are designed to serve high school teachers within a convenient radius. There are some two-dozen *Service Center* meetings throughout the country each year. Their primary purpose is to provide teachers with an opportunity to hear specialists discuss the latest research and writings in their fields and present current, scholarly historical interpretations on selected topics. The sessions are organized to do in person much the sort of thing that is done in the pamphlet series. The conferences have the added benefit of bringing college and research historians directly in touch with the problems and potentials of the school history teacher. Members of the history department at the host institution collaborate with visiting specialists to lead the program sessions. Outside speakers can contribute added interest and broader scope, while the members of the local department or social studies council can provide essential continuity and liaison for ongoing work among college and secondary-school teachers.

THE AMERICAN
HISTORICAL ASSOCIATION

Founded in 1884   Chartered by Congress in 1889

Office: 400 A STREET, S. E., WASHINGTON, D. C. 20003

MEMBERSHIP: Persons interested in historical studies, whether professionally or otherwise, are invited to membership. Present paid membership exceeds 14,000. Members elect the officers by ballot.

MEETINGS: An annual meeting with a three-day program is held during the last days of each year. Many professional historical groups meet within or jointly with the Association at this time. The Pacific Coast Branch holds separate meetings on the Pacific Coast and publishes the *Pacific Historical Review*.

PUBLICATIONS AND SERVICES: The official organ, the *American Historical Review*, is published quarterly and sent to all members. It is available by subscription to others. In addition, the Association publishes its *Annual Report*, prize monographs, pamphlets designed to aid teachers of history, bibliographical as well as other volumes, and the *AHA Newsletter*. To promote history and assist historians, the Association offers many other services. It also maintains close relations with international, specialized, state, and local historical societies through conferences and correspondence.

DUES: There is no initiation fee. Annual regular dues are $15.00, student $7.50 (faculty signature required), and life $300. All members receive the *American Historical Review*, the *AHA Newsletter*, and the program of the annual meeting.

CORRESPONDENCE: Inquiries should be addressed to the Executive Secretary at 400 A Street, S. E., Washington, D. C. 20003.

www.ingramcontent.com/pod-product-compliance
Lightning Source LLC
Chambersburg PA
CBHW031618040426
42452CB00006B/578